CHARLIE'S PARK

THE KITTY CAPER

WRITTEN BY
KIRSTY HOLMES

ILLUSTRATED BY
DRUE RINTOUL

BookLife
freedom

BookLife
PUBLISHING

©2023 BookLife Publishing Ltd.
King's Lynn, Norfolk, PE30 4LS, UK

ISBN 978-1-80505-359-0

A catalogue record for this book is
available from the British Library.

Charlie's Park: The Kitty Caper
Written by Kirsty Holmes
Edited by Robin Twiddy
Illustrated & Designed by Drue Rintoul

Main title font courtesy of Josep.Ng
via Shutterstock.com

ABOUT THE AUTHOR

When she was little, Kirsty knew everything. When it became clear she didn't, she started reading books. Eventually, she realised she would never know everything, and started making things up instead, which is much more fun. Today, she lives mostly in her imagination and hopes you like this story as much as she liked writing it, which is a lot.

ABOUT THE ILLUSTRATOR

Born and raised in King's Lynn, Norfolk, Drue has been a member of the BookLife team for over 8 years, where he has designed and illustrated more than 200 books. He has had a passion for illustration since he was a child, and continues to pursue this love both inside and outside of work. He resides in King's Lynn with his partner, Amy, and their cat, Sprout.

MEET THE CHARACTERS!

Uncle Monty

Charlie

Archie

Chapter 1
Here, Kitty Kitty

The hum of the drone coming through the speakers was soft and buzzy. On the screen, pine trees heavy with snow whizzed across the screen in a blur as the drone flew low and fast. Charlie stuck his tongue out so he could concentrate better.

6

"Careful, Charlie." Uncle Monty waved his arms, both of which were currently bandaged up to the shoulder. Where the bandages ended, Charlie could see a line of circle-shaped bruises running up his skin. Uncle Monty winced. "Ow. Octopus suckers really sting!"

Charlie swooped the drone

controls back and forth in a zig-zag pattern, just like he had practised. The picture on-screen was a bit wobbly, but he was doing OK. Today was the first time Charlie had flown the real drone, but at the moment Uncle Monty couldn't do it. He glanced at his uncle's bandaged arms. And this was really important.

"Focus, Charlie. Keep your eyes on the screen. We need to find Lottie before she has her babies." The snow leopards should have been down the mountain on Tuesday, but Lottie still hadn't returned. Charlie could tell his uncle was worried. "Where could she be?"

Behind them, there was a

whirr, a squeak, and a splash. Archie was working the controls of the Gyroclaw-3000, Uncle Monty's latest invention. Below the Gyroclaw was a large tank of water. In the water, hiding under some rocks, was Maud. Maud was a very grumpy octopus.

Archie narrowed his eyes, and Maud squinted right back

at him.

"I've got you this time."
Archie whispered. The octopus
pouted and drew back. Archie
grasped a joystick in each
hand. Just like in the arcades,
he thought. Aim and CLAW.
He pressed the red button,
and a long metal pole swung
out across the water, stopping
above Maud's head. With a

whirr, a dangling metal arm opened the shiny fingers of its grasping claw. Archie's thumbs flashed and the claw dropped toward the octopus. But Maud was ready, and as the claw dropped, she squeezed her oozy body under

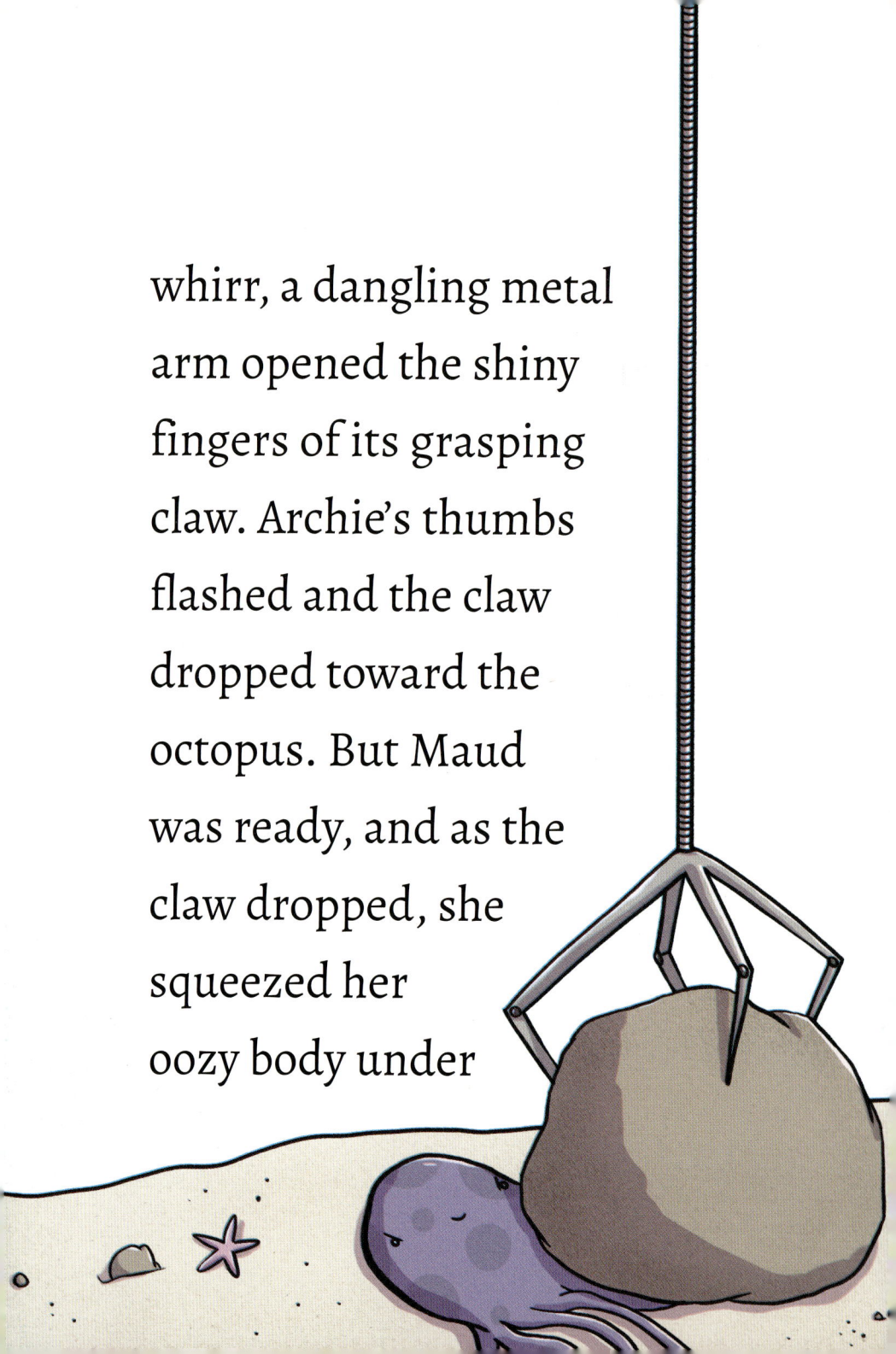

a rock! The claw grabbed the rock, and Maud slipped away.

Again.

"Oof," said Archie. In the arcades, the prizes didn't usually swim away. Maud winked at him from under the rock. Archie lost

his temper and kicked the machine. The claw, wrestling with the heavy rock, squeaked, clanked, then fell off the machine and splashed into the water. Archie sighed and rolled up his sleeve. As he leant into the tank, he stuck his tongue out at Maud.

"Have you caught that grumpy old octopus yet,

Archie my boy?" boomed Uncle Monty from across the room. Archie, holding the dripping claw, shook his head.

"Not yet."

"She's got a very nasty case of the collywobbles. It makes octopuses especially grumpy. If only she would take her medicine – but she's a fighter! Look at the mess she has made

of my arms. Thank goodness for the Gyroclaw 3000. Keep trying, Archie my boy. You'll catch her."

Archie kicked the joystick across the floor. The claw grasped at the air. He stuck them both into his backpack. He'd have to ask Uncle Monty to fix it later.

Chapter 2
Snowed In

Archie wandered over to the screen, watching his big brother skilfully swoop the drone across the snowy landscape. So much snow had fallen in the mountain zone

of the nature park where they lived that the trees looked like snowmen. Huge snow drifts had piled up everywhere, and some of the huge piles of snow were hanging dangerously low. Everything was white.

"Oh – whoops!" said Charlie as the drone wobbled. He fought the controls. The drone spun through the air,

crashing into a small overhang of snow on a rock. Slowly, then all at once, the sheet of snow fell to the ground like a massive pillow. THUMP.

"Careful, Charlie." Uncle Monty said. "The snow is so heavy at this time of year. Any small knock could shake a huge drift loose. If enough falls, it will all slide down the mountain. We don't want to cause an avalanche."

Suddenly, the drone started to beep, and Charlie switched the camera to heat-seeking mode. The screen flashed. Cold areas, such as the freezing snow, were dark purple. The hotter the area became, the brighter and lighter the spot. A small bright dot wobbled across the screen.

"Look, Archie. See that orange hot spot? That's the warm body of a small animal. Probably a squirrel." The hot spot leapt off the screen. The drone swooped onwards.

Suddenly, as they passed some low-hanging trees, a large hot spot appeared. Could it be Lottie? Charlie zoomed in. The blob wobbled and wriggled. As the drone grew closer, the shapes became clearer.

"That's not one hot spot!"

HEAT SEEKING MODE: ON

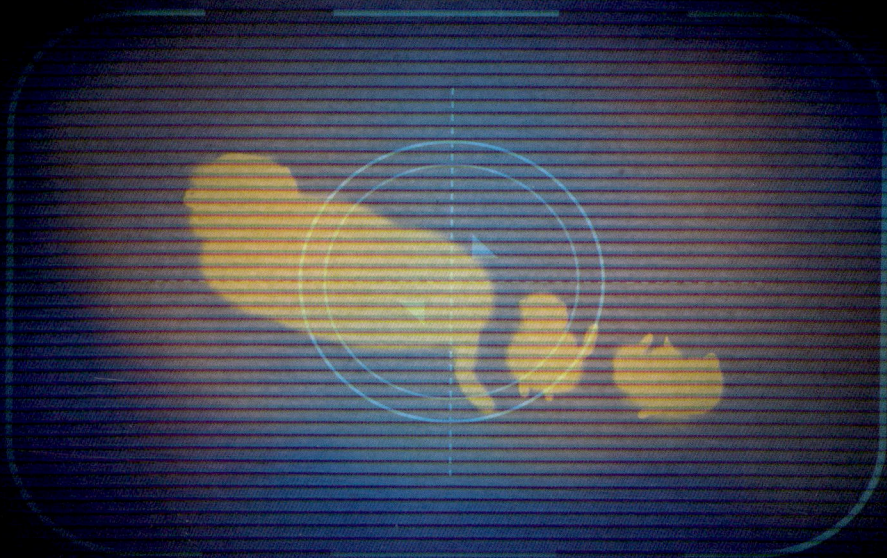

cried Charlie. "It's three!"

"Lottie must have had her babies under there!" said Uncle Monty. "It is very important that we get an emergency new mother pack out to Lottie right away. Then, we need to get both Lottie and her new cubs down the mountain safely and into the cat-ternity hospital where we can take care of them. Boys: we have an emergency on our hands." Uncle Monty looked down at his hands. They were bandaged tightly, like mummified boxing gloves. "Or at least, you boys do."

"We can handle this, Uncle Monty!" said Charlie. "Right, Archie?"

Archie looked at the heat

map on the screen. He did not like the cold. There were a LOT of cold areas in the mountain zone. But Lottie needed help. He nodded.

"I'll need my special winter clothes," he said.

"I knew I could count on you two!" said Uncle Monty.

Time for a rescue mission!

Chapter 3

Hats and Cats

Charlie pulled his backpack off the parked snowmobile. He shivered a little. It was very cold on the mountain. The snow was deep – right up over his knees. He put on his heat vision goggles to look for Lottie and turned around – and jumped back, almost blinded by an enormous bright hot spot.

Charlie ripped off the goggles. In front of him was Archie, wrapped from head to toe in thick, quilted clothing. He was standing in a puddle in a clear area of snow. Steam was coming off him in little ribbons.

"Did you have to wear ALL your heated snow clothes?" Charlie sighed.

Archie nodded. He was very warm and cosy in his heated jumper, coat, gloves, trousers, underpants, hat, socks and, best of all, his

heated boots. He was not cold
at all. Charlie lifted his goggles
and looked around.

"Come on, Arch... This
way," he said. Archie led the
way, his heated suit clearing
a path through the deep snow
for Charlie to follow behind.

Lottie and her cubs were
tucked up under a small group
of trees. The trees, heavy with

snow, had bent over and made a little den, and the three hot spots were snuggled together inside.

"Be careful, Archie," said Charlie. "Look at all that heavy snow on the trees. We mustn't disturb it. Mind the bobble on your hat." Archie took off his hat and dropped it on the ground. They crept carefully

between the branches.

Lottie was curled up in a ball, her thick tail wrapped around her like a fluffy scarf. She narrowed her eyes when the boys appeared, but relaxed when she saw it was Charlie and Archie. She let Charlie pat her on the head, and licked Charlie's

face with her rough tongue.
Then, Lottie slowly moved her
tail aside. Snuggled in very
close to her were two small,
fluffy leopard cubs.

The boys got to work
right away. Archie slipped
new collars onto the cubs and
wrapped Lottie in a warm
blanket. He played with the
babies, tickling them with
the broken claw arm from
his pocket. Charlie used the
walkie-talkie to let the cat-
ternity hospital know they
had found Lottie and were on

their way. Everyone was busy.
So busy, in fact, that no one
noticed the forgotten heated
bobble hat steaming gently
in a puddle outside. No one
noticed when it started to
spark and overheat. And no
one noticed the
snow, melting
a little above
the sparking

bobble hat, starting to slip down the branches.

There was a rumble. A scattering of snow fell across the entrance to the den.

"What was that, Charlie?" said Archie. Lottie lifted her head, picking up the nearest cub in her mouth.

The snow slab above the hat slid off the branch with a

WHOMP.

Oh no.

Avalanche!

Chapter 4
Avalanche!

Charlie, Archie, Lottie and the cubs were swept down the mountain by the tumbling snow. Charlie saw his backpack flying past and managed to grab it, leaping onto it like a toboggan. He rode the backpack down the mountain looking for the others. Archie was just ahead, skidding over the surface in

his heated trousers.

Charlie tried to catch up to his brother, but they were tumbling down the mountain. All around him, snow was flying into the air, creating clouds of frozen flakes. It was hard to make his brother out. The snow was so loud! The falling avalanche rumbled and roared as the snow crashed

down the mountain.

"Archie!" called Charlie.

"I'm here!" yelled Archie through the roar. "I can't reach you!"

"If only your arms were a little longer!" shouted Charlie.

Wait a moment! That was it! Archie did have a longer arm!

"Use the claw!" shouted

Charlie over the roaring snow. "THE CLAW!"

A puff of snow turned his vision white and Archie vanished.

"ARCHIE!" He shouted. Where was he?

The metal claw pierced the cloud of snow, its shiny silver fingers reaching towards him. Charlie grabbed it and pulled.

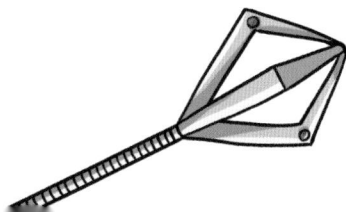

The metal arm was followed by his brother's orange one, and then his bright yellow hair. He pulled Archie onboard the backpack sled.

"It's Ok, Arch." He patted him. "I've got you." Archie held on tight, and they continued to toboggan down the mountain. Where were Lottie and her cubs? It was hard to see in the tumbling snow.

"I see them!" he shouted to Archie. "Get the drone!"

Archie pulled the drone from Charlie's backpack and

quickly fixed the claw arm to the machine. He set it off flying above the racing snow, Charlie steering the backpack closer and closer. Lottie had one cub in her mouth. As they watched, she managed to sink her claws into a tree as she passed, pulling herself and her cub to safety. Phew!

That just left one cub out

there in the snow. Charlie locked onto the hot spot and yanked the backpack hard to the right. They swerved in and out of the trees, chasing the tiny cub down the avalanche. Archie swooped the drone ahead, finally matching the speed of the tumbling cub.

"You can do it, Archie! Just like the arcade!" Charlie

shouted.

Archie took a deep breath, narrowed his eyes, and...

Chapter 5
Grab That Cub

"Missed!" he shouted.

"Try again. Focus... then CLAW!" shouted Charlie.

Archie stuck his tongue out, and focused on the cub, which had rolled itself into a ball and was spinning down the mountainside. All he had to do was grab the cub, but this was harder than catching Maud. Maud wasn't hurtling

down a mountainside at a
million miles an hour. Charlie
swerved the backpack through
some sharp rocks. Archie
pressed the button once more,
and the claw dropped... but the
fur was so fluffy and deep that
the cub slipped through the
claw's metal fingers.

"Erm, Archie?" shouted
Charlie. "I don't want to hurry

you, but…"

Archie looked up from the controls. Oh no.

They were almost at the ravine!

The ravine was deep, full of rocks, and straight ahead. Archie took a deep breath. There was only one more chance to catch the cub before it fell off the edge – or maybe they all did! He HAD to make the catch this time.

He focused on the tiny ball of fur. As it tumbled, the red of its collar flashed. Of course! The collar! Archie knew what he had to do. Charlie steered the backpack, pulling at the straps as hard as he could as the snow slid faster and faster towards the edge of the ravine.

Archie's thumbs flew over the controls in a blur, swooping the drone ahead after the cub.

Lower... lower... almost...

He breathed out, focused on the flash of red, and lowered the drone.

"GOTCHA!"

The claw hooked into the collar, scooping the cub into the air just as the avalanche

flew off the edge of the
ravine.

The cub soared over the
ravine, dangling from its
shiny red collar.
Safe!

"Well done!"
cried Charlie.

"Thanks, Charlie. But, erm... what about us?"

They were still hurtling down the mountain towards the ravine! Charlie swung all his weight hard to the left and skidded the backpack and brothers safely to a halt by some rocks. Charlie sighed. They had done it!

An hour later, Lottie was

curled up in a cabin at the cat-ernity hospital, safe at the foot of the mountain. While Lottie enjoyed a well-deserved rest, Archie and Charlie played with the cubs by the log fire. It was warm in the cabin, and one of the veterinary nurses brought them all hot chocolates. By the time Uncle Monty arrived to pick them

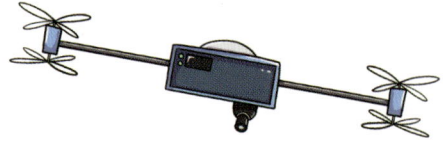

up, the boys were curled up with the cubs by the fire, fast asleep.

Chapter 6

On Solid Ground

The classroom screen flickered, and Lottie appeared with the nurse who had taken care of them after the avalanche. Uncle Monty waved to the nurse. His hand, now out of bandages, was completely fine. Apart from a few sucker-shaped scars, that is.

"Hello, Nurse! How is the

new mother?"

"Lottie is doing brilliantly," said the nurse. "And look who else is here!"

The cubs leapt into view, one on the lap of the nurse and one climbing over Lottie's head.

"You'll never guess what she has named them," said the nurse. "Charlie and Archie!"

Uncle Monty clapped, then winced. "Those tracking devices in their collars mean we won't lose them again. Excellent news all round. Bye for now!" The screen flickered off.

"What a good thing we took the collars with us," said Charlie. "Without them, we might never have caught

Archie the cub!"

"Mmm," said Uncle Monty. "You're right."

They walked over to the tank. Maud was still suffering from the collywobbles and her collies had become wobblier than ever. Someone had put a small mirror in the tank, and Maud was sitting in front of it, posing and admiring herself.

A string of pearls glistened around her neck.

"Is that... a necklace?" said Charlie. Uncle Monty nodded.

"Archie bought her a

present," said Uncle Monty.
Then he giggled. Charlie
raised an eyebrow at his uncle.
What was so funny?

Just then, the machine
arm whizzed out across the
tank. Archie sprang up at the
controls, thumbs flying. The
claw swooped into the tank.
Maud was fast – but not fast
enough. Archie looped the

claw through the necklace and scooped Maud into the air. She was so surprised, her mouth opened in a wide O. Quick as a flash, Uncle Monty pulled a water pistol from his pocket and squirted the collywobble medicine into her mouth.

"She'll feel much better in a day or two. Well done, lad," said Uncle Monty.

Archie gently dropped the octopus back into the pool. She scowled at them and retreated under her favourite rock. A single tentacle appeared behind her, dropping the necklace onto the sand, and then Maud was gone.

Mum's voice crackled over the intercom. "Boys? The